Gallery Books
Editor Peter Fallon

LAMENTATIONS

Paul Muldoon

LAMENTATIONS

Gallery Books

Lamentations
is first published
simultaneously in paperback
and in a clothbound edition
on 23 November 2017.

The Gallery Press
Loughcrew
Oldcastle
County Meath
Ireland

www.gallerypress.com

ISBN 978 1 91133 726 3 *paperback*
978 1 91133 727 0 *clothbound*

A CIP catalogue record for this book
is available from the British Library.

Lamentations receives financial assistance
from the Arts Council.

the arts council
an chomhairle ealaíon
funding literature
artscouncil.ie

Contents

PART ONE

The Churchyard at Creggan

from the Irish of Art Mac Cubhthaigh
(Art McCooey, 1715-1773)

In the churchyard at Creggan I slept, sad as sad, last night,
till a young girl came to me with a kiss at first light;
what with her blush-bright cheek and her hair's golden sheen,
it did my heart good to gaze on that lovely young queen.

'O kind young gentleman, throw off your great sorrow-load
and get up and follow me down the road
to one sweet country the English don't as yet hold in thrall,
where music will lull you from hall to pleasure-hall.'

'O beautiful queen, are you Helen for whom slews were slain
or one of the nine Muses of the Parnassian strain?
In what land were you reared, O unclouded star,
that the likes of myself might consort with your avatar?'

'Don't ask me that question, for to this side of the Boyne I'm
unreconciled,
what with having been reared near Grainneog as a fairy child,
I who elicited in their bard-halls the bards' most lucid tones
of an evening in Tara and by morning in deepest Tyrone.'

'That the O'Neills of Tyrone have left us is my deepest
heart-stab
while their branch in the Fews are restless under their slabs;
those who never turned their backs on the bards, like Niall
Frasach's fresh-faced crew,
but showered us with clothes at Christmas in exchange for a
verse or two.'

'Since the rout of the tribes at Aughrim and the Boyne,
worse luck,
the Irish, who've always stuck by their poets, have themselves
become unstuck.

Wouldn't you be better off in a fairy fort with me by your
flank
than have Williamite arrows hitting your heart point-blank?'

'I wouldn't leave for all the gold that went with the kings to
their mounds.
I'm loath to leave my friends who're still above ground,
never mind my wife to whom I promised so much when she
was young.
Were I to desert her now I know she'd be sorrow-stung.'

'You don't have a single relative who's still alive and well.
You're piss-poor, penniless, a hollow-eyed hallion without a
hope in Hell.
Wouldn't you be better off with a girl with a soft touch
than have these so-and-sos come down hard on your poems
as such?'

'O beautiful young queen, though falling for you's been my
fate,
I won't go down that road unless you stipulate
that, be it on the Shannon, the Isle of Man, or in Egypt I die,
it's in my own sweet-smelling churchyard at Creggan I'll lie.'

PART TWO

The Lament for Art O'Leary

A reimagining of *Caoineadh Airt Uí Laoghaire*
by Eibhlín Dubh Ní Chonaill
(18th century)

Music established and held under

EILEEN My fast friend, my stalwart.
Firmest of the firm.
At the Market House in the cattle mart
I first took in your form.
There was a gleam in my eye.
A glimmer in my heart.
I left my own people by and by
and ran away with you, Art.

Music out

Not once did I look back.
The parlors freshly whitewashed.
The rooms beautifully appointed.
The oven aglow
and a batch of loaves ready to go.
Roasts turning on their spits
now the cattle were butchered.
I would sleep in eiderdown
till noon milking time came round,
or later if I wanted.

ART'S SISTER You brought cattle as a keepsake,
Eileen, but no dowry of gold coin.
Yet you would sleep in eiderdown
till noon milking time came round.

EILEEN My stalwart, my fast friend.
What comes to mind
of that fine Spring day
was the alluring tilt

of your hat's gold band,
your sword's silver hilt,
your manly right hand,
your demeanour so confident
it left your two-faced foes
quaking in their boots.
As you got ready to mount
your lithe, white-faced steed
the Englishmen bowed down
to the ground, not because
they held you in proper esteem,
but out of sheer funk.
You died, my sweetheart,
because of those same punks.

ART'S FATHER Bad cess to you, Abraham Morris.
May misfortune hit you hard!
Bad cess to you, Abraham Morris,
for the taking of my son, Art.

EILEEN My fair-handed horseman!
They became you, the bodkin
pinned deep under your cambric,
and your hat fringed with lace.
After your return from Austria
passersby made way for you
not with a kind word
but outright contempt.

My fast friend! My stalwart!
When they do come home,
our little pet, Conor,
and our babe-in-arms, Fiach,
they'll ask at once
where I left their father.

I'll have to tell them, sadly,
I left him in Kilnamartyra.
They'll call out for their daddy.
They'll get no response.
My fast friend! My little calf!
You who claimed kin with the Earl of Antrim
and the Barrys of Inchigeelagh!
How they became you, the sword-blade,
the hat under its band,
the fashionably narrow shoe
and, sure enough,
the suit made of imported stuff.

ART'S FATHER Bad cess to you, Abraham Morris!
May misfortune hit you hard.
May you go stone-blind.
May your joints be jolted and jarred.

EILEEN My stalwart! My fast friend!
Little did I think you might be dead
till your mare arrived home
with her reins trailing the ground,
your life-blood drenching her broad croup
as far as the gleaming saddle
where you'd sit or stand in the stirrups.
One leap carried me over the threshold,
a second brought me to the gateway,
a third as far as the horse herself.
I slapped my hands smartly
and galloped off
just as quickly as I was able.
I would find you stretched
by that little bit of a whin bush
without Pope or bishop
or clergy of any sect

to give you the last rites
but, *faute de mieux*, some wizened old doll
who had covered you in her shawl.
Your blood was still a gush.
I made no attempt to staunch it.
I cupped my palms and drank it.

Music established and held under

My fast friend! My stalwart!
Would you ever rouse yourself
and come back home with me?
The fatted calf I'll have them kill.
I'll lay on a huge feast
with the liveliest of music.
I'll prepare a bed for you
with bright sheets
and fine patchwork quilts
that'll bring you out in a sweat
and rid you of this chill you've caught.

Music out

ART'S SISTER My brother! My treasure!
There are any number of shapely women
between the quays of Cork
and the bridge at Toom
who could have brought not only cattle as a keepsake
but a dowry of gold coin —
women who wouldn't have fallen asleep in their room
on the night of your wake.

EILEEN My fast friend! My lamb!
Pay no heed to any of them.
They're nothing more than scandal mongers.
As for that jealous man's tittle-tattle
about my nodding off,
I put my head down only
because your babies were rattled
and I had to attend
to getting them settled.
My nearest and dearest,
there's not a woman in Ireland
could lie down beside him
as the sun itself went down
and bear him three youngsters
who wouldn't lose it entirely
after losing Art O'Leary,
Art who was left *hors de combat*
only yesterday morning.

Music established and held under

ART'S FATHER Bad cess to you, little Abraham Morris,
may misfortune hit you hard.
May you go stone-blind.
May your joints be jolted and jarred.
You who poleaxed my son,
my boy-calf,
and left not a single Irishman
willing to fire a shot on his behalf.
My fast friend! My sweetheart!
Would you ever pay me a little heed?
Would you ever get up, Art,
and leap onto your steed?
Would you ever head back to Inchigeelagh
by way of beautiful Macroom

with your grasp on a bottle of wine as firm
as it used to be in your daddy's front room?

Music out

EILEEN It's my greatest cause for sorrow
I couldn't be at your side
when the bullet was fired
so it lodged in my own right flank
or the edge of my chemise,
O my master horseman, my Hussar,
while you headed for the hills.
My master horseman, my Hussar,
while you headed for the hills.

ART'S SISTER It's my own greatest regret
I didn't have your back
when the gun went off.
I'd have taken the hit in my own waist
or the hem of my dress
even as you made your escape,
my grey-eyed rider,
taking everything in your scope.
O my grey-eyed rider,
taking everything in your scope.

EILEEN My dear friend! My sweetheart!
What ugly, ill-fitting attire for a hero —
the coffin and the death-cap
set on a great-hearted horseman
who was given to fishing in streams
and drinking in big houses
in the company of white-breasted women.
No wonder my head is in a spin
now I've lost my lynchpin.

Damn you to hell, Abraham Morris,
you plug-ugly backstabber.
You took the man of my house
and the father of my youngsters —
two of them toddlers
and the third still in my womb,
unlikely now to be delivered.

Music established and held under

My friend! My shining one!
You were no sooner out the gate
than you'd be back again,
kissing both your children,
kissing the tips of my fingers
and saying, 'Eileen, get up
and finish your work
post haste
for I'm leaving home
and may come back only in a coffin.'
I tended to respond with a smirk
for you talked this way so often.
My friend! My own one!
My bright-bladed rider!
Up you get right now
and put on your spotless suit
of the finest weave.
Put on your hat of black beaver.
Put on your riding gloves.
Your whip is ready to fall.
Your mare is primped and primed.
Take that narrow road east
where the bushes will turn aside for you
and the stream narrow in your path
and men and women will bow

if they've any manners at all —
though I fear most don't at the present time.

Music out

My true love! My best company!
It's not to my own people who've died —
not the three babies I lost
nor Donal Mór Ó Connell
nor Conal who was lost at sea
nor that young woman of twenty-six
who spent so much time abroad
consorting with royalty —
it's not to them I appeal
but Art, cut down last night
on the water meadow of Carriganimmy.
The rider of the brown mare
lying there all on his lonesome,
no living creature to tend to him
but those little mill-women dressed in black.
To make matters worse, I fear,
they couldn't bring themselves to shed a tear.
My fast friend! My pet!
O Art O'Leary,
son of Conor, son of Ceadach,
son of Laoiseach O'Leary,
west from The Gearagh
and east from the Caolchnoc
where mountain berries
and yellow nuts grow on the branches
and the apple-trees are weighed down
when harvest time comes round —
should anyone truly be taken aback
to find the O'Leary lands set ablaze
along with Ballingeary

and Gougane Barra of the saints
on account of a rider so adroit
he'd outrun the Grenagh hunt
leaving the hounds stopped in their tracks
after their tremendous exertions?
O my glad-eyed horseman,
what ever befell you last night?
I suppose I must have convinced myself
you'd never come to harm
when I splashed out on your fancy uniform.

Music established and held under

ART'S SISTER My fast friend! My darling dear!
So much a part of the ruling class
you had eighteen nursemaids at any given time.
Think of the riches they'd amass —
a brood mare, a milch cow,
a sow and her farrow-fold,
a grist-mill on a ford,
a hoard of silver and gold,
a piece of land by way of estate,
fine velvet and even finer silks.
You were the calf to whom those wet nurses
offered their breasts spouting milk.
My darling! Mystery of my heart!
My pet! My shining pigeon!
Though I couldn't be with you in the flesh
nor bring any of my family retainers
that shouldn't bring disgrace or derision
given how they're all under duress
in their closed-off rooms
and their snug coffins,
sleeping the sleep from which there's no waking.

Music out

My fast friend! My calf!
Last night in Cork, at a very late hour,
as I lay in a trance
in bed on my lonesome,
I was offered a vision.
Our whitewashed mansion had fallen,
The Gearagh itself was a wasteland.
There wasn't a whiffle from our lean hounds.
The birds didn't make the slightest sound
now you'd been ambushed
in the middle of the mountains over beyond
with no priest, no clergyman,
but that fierce old biddy
covering you with the peak of her mantle
where you were pinned to the ground,
Art O'Leary,
your blood so blatant, so unabashed,
running down the front of your shirt.
My love and my darling!
How well they became you,
your stockings at least five-ply,
your riding boots at least knee-high,
your Caroline hat worn at a rakish angle
and the lash of your whip
on your spunky gelding
and all those maidens, so meek and so mild,
sizing you up from behind.

Music established and held under

EILEEN Dearest of the dear! My stalwart! My steadfast one!
When you strode through the market towns

that are themselves steadfast and slavish
the very shopkeepers' wives
would offer you a curtsey,
for they recognized immediately
your great prowess as a bed-mate,
as a front runner on horseback,
as a father of children.
Sweet Jesus himself is well aware
there'll be no outlay on a cap to cover my head
nor underthings pressed against my flank
nor new shoe on my foot
nor any new items of furniture about the house
nor a bit of harness on the brown mare
that I'll not use instead to fund my lawsuit;
for I'll go across the ocean
to present King George with a petition,
and if he won't pay me any heed
I'll be back *tout de suite*
to face that black-blooded brute
who robbed me of what I most valued.

Music out

ART'S SISTER My love! My shining star!
You were just another of the rough riders
hunting high and low in the glen
till you turned them around
and brought them back to the big house.
There knives were given a fresh edge
the better to carve pork.
The mutton would be sufficient unto the day
along with those heavy-headed, red oats
that make horses snort —
those same horses, rangy and unkempt
despite their grooms being to hand.

Even if those huntsmen stayed for a week
you'd never think to charge for their beds
or their horses' fodder,
O my brother, my belovèd brother.

EILEEN My love! My darling!
I now hold them in the highest regard,
the women of the mill, so fine and fair,
and the excellence of their lamentations
for the rider of the brown mare.
Would that my cries might be heard
as far as Derrynane
or Capling of the yellow apples.
Then many a bonny light horseman
and many a girl with a spotless white
handkerchief
would be here *tout de suite*
to shed tears all the while
over Art O'Leary, Art of the ready smile.

ART'S SISTER Were it not for the smallpox
and the Black Death
and the spotted fever
my own rough and ready band of riders
would be rattling their reins
and raising a rumpus
even as they prepared to lay you to rest,
O Art of the resplendent breast.

EILEEN As for you, Seán Cooney,
may you rot in hell, you twister.
Since you're a fellow given to taking a bribe
you might have brought it to my attention.
I could have offered you quite a lot —
a thick-coated horse

to bear you away through the pressing throng
on the day of your greatest hardship,
cattle as far as the eye could see,
sheep dropping lambs for you,
a gentleman's suit
complete with spurs and high boots —
though I must say I'd regret
seeing you got up in them
for I'm pretty sure I've heard tell
you should be known as Mister Puny.
Mister Piss-poor. Mister Prickster.
O my rider of the white hands,
now your hand has been laid low
I want you to get up and go
to James Baldwin's house.
That plug-ugly landlord,
that bow-legged louse.
I want you to demand satisfaction
for the loss of your mare
and the wasting away of your bright love.
May Baldwin and his six children fade and
fester!
I mean no harm to his wife, Máire,
though there's no love lost between us
despite the fact my own mother's body
held each of us for three trimesters.

Music established and held under

My fast friend, dearest of the dear.
The one I love the most.
Your yellow corn's stacked high and dry,
your cows are at their posts . . .
And yet my grief so weighs me down
it's not something the men of Munster could lift.

It's not something the blacksmiths of Oileán
na bhFionn
would be able to shift.
My fast friend, dearest of the dear.
Would that you might be here.
My fast friend, dearest of the dear.
Would that you might still be here.

ART'S SISTER The brood mare, Art, and the milch-cow,
the sow and her farrow-fold,
the grist-mill on the ford,
the hoard of silver and gold,
the piece of land by way of estate,
fine velvet and even finer silks.
You were the calf to whom those wet-nurses
offered their breasts spouting milk.
My fast friend, dearest of the dear.
Would that you might still be here.

EILEEN Till Art O'Leary will come back
my grief won't be assuaged.
My grief has grown till it's so big
it crushes my ribcage . . .
It seems that now my heart has sunk
under the weight of grief that's been shut away
in one of those padlocked chests, or a padlocked
trunk,
and the key gone astray.
My fast friend, dearest of the dear.
Would that you might be here.
My fast friend, dearest of the dear.
Would that you might still be here.

ART'S FATHER My fast friend! My sweetheart!
Would you ever pay me a little heed?

Would you ever get up, Art,
and leap onto your steed?
Would you ever head back to Inchigeelagh
by way of beautiful Macroom
with your grasp on a bottle of wine as firm
as it used to be in your daddy's front room?
My fast friend, dearest of the dear.
Would that you might still be here.

EILEEN The women keening there beyond
should raise their *cri de coeur*
till Art calls for another pint
and one more for the poor . . .
Till Art enters that great enclave,
that underground school where he goes not to hone
his skill with stanzas of verse, or musical staves,
but to stave off earth and stone.
My fast friend, dearest of the dear.
Would that you might still be here.

Music out

ALL My fast friend, dearest of the dear.
Would that you might still be here.

Black

PART THREE

Songs from Ben Gunn

All at Sea

I was born and bred in Fermanagh
On the shores of Lough Erne
By six I was an orphan
There was nowhere I could turn
I was taken in by my uncle
The poet Cathal Buí
He spoke to me *as Gaeilge*
I learned Irish at his knee
Till I was eleven years of age
From there I went to Sligo
And the Sligo quay
The future had seemed unclouded
Till I shook from stem to stern
Wave upon wave had flown into a rage
And I found myself at sea
I found myself all at sea

I set sail on the *Walrus*
With Jack Flint at the helm
Hallions all . . . hellraisers
Disturbing the peace of the realm
When I left Bristol harbour
In 1743
I paid no more heed to Silver's limp
Than any amputee
From Blackbeard to Barbarossa
For tearing men limb from limb
Was meat and drink to me
To give up riproaring to give up robbery
Would have left me overwhelmed
Would have left me at a loss
Would have left me all at sea
With the Welshman Pew who lost his sight
When a cannon burst its breech
And whom I'd promised to lead right

To the treasure buried on the beach
When I failed to deliver the chest of gold
I was first tortured by Israel Hands
Then thrown in chains in the hold
Then set down on a foggy spit of sand
Where it seemed I was destined
To end my days with McPhee and Preston

I never took the time to mourn
Those who live on despite a fatal wound
Or think how many a mariner
Must find himself marooned
Till I woke in that miasma
With Preston and McPhee
Jack Silver had stabbed my messmates
During a drunken spree
Preston was blood-bearded blood-quiffed
And when McPhee went junglewards
I was left without company
Though I stood there on firm shingle
I slowly became attuned
To the fact I had been cast adrift
To the fact I was at sea
The fact I was all at sea

Goat Dance

One year I spent trying to creep
Up on the goats while they were asleep
In the little copse I called Madrid
It was the spot
Where they held court
And had something akin to sport
A she-goat and her little Captain Kidd
Were dancing a gavotte
When the she-goat gave a leap
With a huppity-huppity-hup
For she knew the jig was up

One year I spent finecombing a cap
Of goatskin so the nap
Would throw off the rain
As befits an old salt
The fact that my coat
Had been worn by a billy goat
Meant he hadn't died in vain
As he waltzed
Into my pitfall trap
With a huppity-huppity-hup
When he knew the jig was up

One year I spent counting the vast
Treasure Flint had amassed
And buried on Spy-
glass Hill
Till that fateful day
The tenth of May
Three goats and I
Were dancing a quadrille
When we heard a ship's cannon blast
With a huppity-huppity-hup
And we knew the jig was up

Got Away from Me

Once I prayed to God
For a taste of salt cod
Or cheddar cheese
A pickled plum
A nip of rum
A biscuit crumb
The bird I hoped to snare
Took to the air
From the palm tree
It got away from me
It got away
It got away from me

From their sandbar
My fellow tars
Had made mournful pleas
I heard them beg
For a powder keg
From Jack the Peg
I was about to make a point
About the artificial joint
And piracy
It got away from me
It got away
It got away from me

When I came back to England
After years of godlessness
I tried to disentangle
Myself from that unholy mess
I gave up the sea surge
For the love of Margaret Bundy
I gave up Captain Teach
For the school Meg taught on Sundays

When I came back to England
After years of being rudderless
I tried to disentangle
Myself from my sculdudderies
I gave up compass for compassion
A twist of tobacco for whist
I gave up the navy ration
For a nave lying at a list
I gave up Blind Pew for a pew in church
Salt cod for the psalter
Even marriage seemed within reach
Till Meg left me at the altar
She got away from me
Get away she said
You get away from me

She must have seen I'd lost faith
In coming alongside her staithe
And mooring in her lee
In lying in her sheltered cove
Never more to rove
In search of treasure trove
The possibility I once divined
Of Ben Gunn becoming refined
The possibility of feeling benign
Towards Silver and his kind
And Grace one day being mine
Had tugged on my line
Then suddenly broke free
It got away from me
It got away
It got away from me

That's why I'm heaving to
That's why I'm going to fetch

That goatskin parasol
From my old sea chest
I'll put together a crew
And set out afresh
For the coast of Hy-brasil
The Islands of the Blest

PART FOUR

Songs from Typhoid Mary

Long Cookstown (1906)

As I was coming through Long Cookstown
Nancy Whiskey I chanced to spy . . .
The last night I would spend in Ireland
I heard that song for the very first time
A boy falls victim to hard liquor
A woman of easy virtue
A frosty night in mid-November
That hill's a cake left out to cool
At the hiring fair in Long Cookstown
He was hired out the first of May
The life of a servant boy in Ireland
Is little better than a slave's
But he didn't mind getting his hands dirty
He's worked six months he's earned six pounds
Now he's spent it all on Nancy Whiskey
Now he's come back to Long Cookstown

When I grew up in Long Cookstown
That was the life that lay in store
A servant girl to a hardfaced farmer
A straw bed on the stable floor
To Tullyhogue we'd head most Sundays
The royal site of the O'Neills
My kith and kin had died of hunger
In those selfsame potato fields
Though it was in the 1840s
We'd borne the brunt of the disease
The potato fields of Connaught
Still suffered blight in the 70s
I've traded Cookstown for Long Island
Swapped Tullyhogue for Cutchogue
The farmers here all grow potatoes
Their flowers more lovely than a rose
To Tullyhogue we'd head most Sundays
To see where the O'Neills were crowned

Our own progress was almost regal
As we walked back to Long Cookstown

My childhood was dull as dishwater
A thatched roof under which we'd sit
With only stirabout to eat
Some nights I listened to the music
Where pots lined up to catch more drips
Some nights that music tasted sweet . . .

As I was coming through Long Cookstown
Nancy Whiskey I chanced to spy . . .
Now I've ended up in Long Island
As a house cook to the quality
Mrs Warren and I are planning supper
We've finalized tonight's menu
The only thing left undecided
Will it be blancmange? Will it be fool?
Isinglass is made of the swim bladder
Of sturgeon or Atlantic cod
The stuff I use to set a blancmange
May help me stiffen my resolve
Mrs Warren wants blancmange for pudding
And I've run out of isinglass
But I've a plan that's copper-bottomed
I've a plan that's iron-cast
Mrs Warren knows that I'm resourceful
That a solution will be found
I'll substitute beef gelatin
I'll put the cook back in Long Cookstown

Clams (1906)

Mrs Warren hired me on the first of May
And brought me out to Oyster Bay
And her summer rental
Peaches and ice cream
Were Mrs Warren's constant themes
She also brought a couple of maids
And a gardener with a braid
I took for an Oriental

Ten years of living in the States
Have seen me acclimate
To things that once seemed foreign
I've learned to bake candied yams
And clove-studded country ham
Ten years of being salt-cured
Have also left me inured
To the likes of Mrs Warren

Now her daughters and two maids
And Sam the Braid
Have come down with typhoid fever
Making a splash
With its rosy rash
Now Mrs Warren has her own
Spots on her breastbone
Like blood spots on a cleaver

It's been like this since the first of May
When we came out to Oyster Bay
And the summer rental
It wasn't my gooseberry fool
Gave them their pea-green stool
The fact that the maids and Sam
Have been eating local clams
Is hardly coincidental

I'll Run You Through (1907)

You rip you rapscallion
You gulpin you glipe
Don't come next or near Mary Mallon
Or I'll cut out your tripes

You tinker's get you tatterdemalion
You gommeril you gobshite
If you come next or near Mary Mallon
I'll cut out your liver and lights

You hoor you hallion
I'll knock you into a bag of blue
Don't come anywhere next or near Mary Mallon
Or I'll run you through

A Guest of the City (1907)

I was minding my own business
On Park Avenue
When that poisonous
George Soper first hove into view
Since Mrs Warren cut my recompense
I'd taken two more jobs
The Kesslers and the Bowens
Two families with whom I hobnobbed
Over ice cream and peaches
Now George Soper wanted to test
My urine and faeces
Though I tried my very best
To stop him from doing his dirty work
Soper's the reason I've become a guest
Of the City of New York
Yes I've become a special guest
Of the City of New York

When they sent an ambulance
And five policemen to nab
Me I upset their plans
By taking a stab
At Miss Baker of the Department of Health
Miss Josephine Baker pinned my wings
And pushed me down into the filth
Though they didn't send me to Sing Sing
They have sent me up the East River
They say I resisted arrest
Did Miss Baker expect me to roll over?
I threatened to stab her in the chest
With a carving fork
That's partly how I became a guest
Of the City of New York
Yes that's how I became a special guest
Of the City of New York

Tonight in Washington DC
George Soper is giving a talk about me
In which he'll claim
I am to blame
And should be brought to book
For people getting sick in houses where I cooked
In 1900 in Mamaroneck
In 1901 in Manhattan
In 1902 in Dark Harbor
In 1904 in Sands Point
In 1906 in Oyster Bay
In 1906 in Tuxedo Park
In 1907 in Manhattan again
He won't mention that I myself am right as rain
He'll be taking a bow
Without having mentioned how

I was minding my own business
In the privy at 688 Park
When His Bossiness
George Soper broke in to barrack
Me about my part
In leaving 22 people sick
One of them dead and buried
Now the main dish at the picnic
Is my own head on a platter
Tonight he'll have once more professed
It's in my gallbladder
A terrible pest
Is supposed to lurk
Like an uninvited guest
Of the City of New York
The typhoid that's made me a special guest
Of the City of New York

Hell's Kitchen (1908)

As I roved out in the West Fifties
In 1895
I found myself in Hell's Kitchen
Among my own kind

The screams from behind shutters
Clotheslines flecked with soot
Urine standing in puddles
Rain dripping through the roof

The riff-raff and the rowdies
Peep shows and pimps
The junkshops and wharfhouses
All raising a stink

Amidst the filthy and depraved
The women of low repute
Sat Mr August Breihof
Drinking on a stoop

I taught August how to bake a gateau
He taught me the cakewalk
Soon we were going steady
High stepping through New York

Here on North Brother (1909)

More than 1000 people drowned
When the *General Slocum* ran aground
On this island in the East River
The fact they were burned alive
Or drowned when they dived
Still gives me the shivers
Even a single
Measure of rum may mingle
With a smidgin of grenadine
But I'm doomed
To a living tomb
To be in quarantine
In a pigsty
A pig may lie
Down with another
A one-room bungalow
Is all I know
Here on North Brother

Even though I've committed no crime
I find myself doing time
In near isolation
Three times a day a keeper appears
With food then flees for fear
Of contamination
Even an East River porpoise
Has recourse to *habeas corpus*
They call me a healthy carrier
The way they leave food at my door
Makes me think I'm no more
Than a fox terrier
Though I've been tied
Here like a dog I've tried
Not to get in a pother
I trust the good Lord

Will make a scourge of cords
And free me from North Brother

I'm a woman
That's a mark against me
I'm unmarried
That's a mark against me
I'm Catholic
That's a mark against me
I'm Irish
That's surely a mark against me
I'd be far better off
A servant girl
Like Biddy Duff
Or Mary McCarroll
With pigs to swill
And cattle to fother
Than held against my will
Here on North Brother

They treat me as if I'm some kind of a thug
It's hooey it's humbug
It's hogwash it's hokum
It's as if I might
Be responsible for the plight
Of the *General Slocum*
Even a cakewalker even a high stepper
Can end up a leper
In Riverside Hospital
The fact that I knock
Over any stumbling block
Is itself an obstacle
If I were making a mint
And not a poor immigrant
I wouldn't be having this bother

The court has ruled today
That I must stay
Here on North Brother

Free (1910)

In the name of all that's merciful this is the first
Time since I met that accursed
George Soper I've thought I might burst
Into song
I've put my memories of being outcast
My memories of being harassed
Back into the past
Where they belong
I'm no longer a skivvy
Hiding in a privy
And trying to chivvy
Myself along
I'm free
I'm free
I'm free at last

My lawyer George O'Neill has the common touch
Despite his coming from a long line of kings and such
He helped me take Josephine Baker and much
More in my stride
The judge looked aghast
At the so-called evidence she amassed
Her public lambastes
How she libelled me how she lied
Though the suspicion lingers
Soper or one of his dead ringers
Will want to go sticking a finger
Into my side
I'm free
I'm free
I'm free at last

To ride two abreast on a carousel
Where the Coney Island elephant once stood
To see Ota Benga and his orang-utang

Up at the Bronx Zoo
To hear the mallet men ring their bell
On the clock in Herald Square
And not to feel the slightest pang
As I take the enchanting East River air

In the name of all that's holy I'll hear no talk of bugs
Or urotropin and those other drugs
Or gallbladder removal from Soper and the mugs
Who've tried to open my every vein
My confidence is vast
My inner strength is unsurpassed
And I'm steadfast
Against the man who's caused me pain
I've made a promise
To that Doubting Thomas
I've made a promise
I won't cook again
I'm free
I'm free
I'm free at last

Recapture (1916)

At the time President Taft
Was slung like a pig on a hook
I signed the affidavit
I'd not hire out as a cook

I found work in laundries
For a couple of years
Up alleyways and stinking entries
I kept myself in the clear

It was like committing heresy
That washerwoman stuff
The starch I'd once washed out of rice
I now put back into cuffs

In smoothing cuffs and collars
I worked my hands raw
The mystery most glorious
Was how August forgave my flaws

I sued the city for damages
My income was so low
Even though I was tenacious
They didn't want to know

We would gad about we would gallivant
Myself and my dear August
Until in May 1911
He would return to dust

Shortly after that I registered
With Mrs Stricker's agency
I was back making custard
I was back making beef tea

Before long I was working
At Sloane Maternity Hospital
All those doctors and nurses
Dredging the birth canal

I'd registered at Mrs Stricker's
Under the name Mary Brown
When 25 nurses and doctors
Suddenly came down

With typhoid fever
This time two of them died
I was quickly recaptured
I had nowhere to hide

In Dublin this past Easter
Our backs were to the wall
We rose up against the Britishers
To whom we've been in thrall

Now I've been recaptured
I'm back in my bungalow
I'm back here on North Brother
Back in my own peep show

Ireland will have her freedom
The banner's been unfurled
I'm a byword for confinement
Through the whole wide world

I'm a byword for contagion
A mad dog at large
All the water in the ocean
Won't clear me of this charge

North Brother Blues (1938)

The lapwing causes a diversion
She trails one wing along the ground
The lapwing causes a diversion
She trails one wing along the ground
The lapwing limps in the other direction
So her nest will not be found

My progress used to be quite queenly
Those Sundays back from Tullyhogue
My progress used to be quite queenly
Those Sundays back from Tullyhogue
Now I keep pace with Ma Rainey
On the Sunday gramophone

Her songs are full of resentment
Her songs are raised like fists
Her songs are full of resentment
Her songs are raised like fists
They go back to the plantation
They go back to her master's voice

A dog's been my companion
On North Brother these thirty years
Three dogs have been my companions
On North Brother these thirty years
Only when its wings are pinioned
Does a bird sing loud and clear

My music's the music of rainwater
Through the holes in a thatched roof
The music of rainwater
Dripping through a roof
This last night I'll spend on North Brother
Is my last night on earth

A stroke has left me lopsided
My face is out of true
A stroke has left me lopsided
My face is out of true
The day I started back in that hospital
Is a day I've come to rue

The lapwing causes a diversion
She trails one wing along the ground
The lapwing causes a diversion
She trails one wing along the ground
There'll be no more talk of infection
When I come back through Long Cookstown

PART FIVE

Olagón

Pillow Talk

I long Medhbh for the nights I could ply
My trade between your thighs
And not have to put up with the lies
Of some *bean an tí* from Navan

The pundit Ivan O'Pinion
Claims the British have no more dominion
Over us than the Virginians
And I don't mean Virginia, Cavan

I long for the nights
When everything still felt right
I know I no longer need to prove myself
By running along a chariot-pole like an elf
It no longer behooves me

O Medhbh Medhbh we were just so
Till you went on *The Late Late Show*
And shared our home movies

When you declared yourself cock of the walk
And made public our pillow talk
Pillow talk, pillow talk, made public our pillow talk

I long Ailíll for the days we'd operate a sting
On the political wing
With the help of Dawn and Spring
And their Father Major O'Ffensive

Before the Navan *fear an tí*
Detected an irregularity
In how we'd registered the charity
That left us all quite pensive

I long for the days
When our love still held sway
I know you'd still much prefer to think
It's the pills and the drink
That make me drowsy
Ailíll Ailíll we were just so
Till you forced me to go on that *Táin Bó*
Against the northern bowsies

Now we'll both need a bit of electroshock
If you don't pay heed to my pillow talk
Pillow talk, pillow talk, pay heed to my pillow talk.

Níl aon tinteán mar do thinteán féin
There's no place like home
Is biorach intinn an mhic leinn
The hornet eats the honey comb
Tugann Tadhg an dá thaobh
Cul le gach cuis
One card up the sleeve
Is worth two in the bush
Is fearr, a chroí, is fearr
Aon crann na dhá úll
Every bridge is a bridge too far
Every chorus a chorus of disapproval

I long Medhbh for the nights when whether I'd seek
And destroy or turn the other cheek
On that two-faced Fergus O'Blique
Was still a toss-up
That while I was captain of the vanity
I had sexual relations with a manatee
Is a rumour spread by the Cavan *bean an tí*
And her son Colum the Gossip
I long for the nights

When I was still a sprite
I know I don't run like lightning along a chariot-pole
But I still want to rock your gypsy soul
Like Van in *Into the Mystic*
You were just so, Medhbh,
Till you went to that rave
With Nessa and Niamh Ní Hilistic
Though your gypsy soul I still want to rock
After we're through with our pillow talk
Pillow talk pillow talk through with our pillow talk

1

Now Queen Medhbh had brought me in
Ar scáth a chéile a mhaireas na daoine
And made me tea out of her wee tin
While she drank vodka martinis
Then like a *spéirbhean* had flown
Ochón agus ochón ó
Into what used to be a no-fly zone
Ochón agus ochón ó

The sky-woman flies by private jet
But speaks a garble of Gaelic and Greek
Medhbh confessed that her cap was set
At the activist Fergus O'Blique
Her husband Ailíll now slept alone
Ochón agus ochón ó
(He'd always been depression prone)
Ochón agus ochón ó

Fergus O'Blique favoured heavy ham-hocks
And head-on confrontations
He modelled himself on Papa and Baby Doc
When it came to creating a nation
In an image not unlike his own
Ochón agus ochón ó
For not all terrorism is homegrown
Ochón agus ochón ó

Manus Machination favoured the dead letter box
Over the live round
Medhbh raised her whiskey on the rocks
To gunrunners running aground
Her heroes were Emmet and Wolfe Tone
Ochón agus ochón ó

Bold Robert Emmet . . . Theobald Wolfe Tone . . .
Ochón agus ochón ó

Medhbh's singleminded doublespeak
Was no less a distortion
Than when Manus Machination and Fergus O'Blique
Vied for the champion's portion
Both would ham it up on that ham-bone
Ochón agus ochón ó
One or other must be overthrown
Ochón agus ochón ó

2

Now Medhbh had given up her king
O'Blique took her under his wing
And made her a co-signatory
She signed her name
To what he proclaimed
The Republic of Futurity
Being only a dame
She was only fair game
For being plucked from obscurity

He was no mere watchdog
Rolling a log
Like a wave rolling out a big dory
She tried hard to ignore
His tidal bore
Of data on ethnic purity
Blue-eyed and blond
His word was his bond
In the sense of a surety

As for dealing horse
He was more or less forced
By his uncle Bertie O'Bligatory
It was all a blur
To a mean cur
Who moonlighted in private security
O'Blique's premature
Climaxes she was sure
Were a function of his demurity

And nothing more deep-rooted

3

Though she insisted she was on lemonade
Medhbh had seemed a little tiddly
When she came back from the cattle raid
She'd christened '*Táin Bó* Diddley'
She was more than a little accident prone
Ochón agus ochón ó
After a bottle or two of Côtes du Rhone
Ochón agus ochón ó

Night was set to go twelve rounds with day
Both had turned semi-professional
Now Ailíll entered the fray
As Ireland went recessional
Tá 'n deachracht ceangailte leis an Dow Jones
Ochón agus ochón ó
A queen bee will disembowel a drone
While dabbing herself with *eau de cologne*

Now Medhbh relied on prescription drugs
Like Fergus O'Blique on the tonton

You can sweep almost anything under the rug
When you're high on the OxyContin
She claimed was less stolen than on extended loan
Ochón agus ochón ó
But throughout it all I heard Ailíll groan
Ochón agus ochón ó

4

For aeons and aeons
Our names were in neon
Tá sé go hiontach
Ach is minic a bhionn
Ciúin ciontach

The ones who are quiet
Incite the riots
But Tate & Lyle (i.e. toot)
Is the staple diet
Of the Tonton Macoute

In the great mingle-mangle
Is minic cuma aingeal
Ar an diabhail féin
It's hard so hard to wrangle
The needle from the vein

Once Ailíll gave no quarter
To the arms importer
Seán 'Von Braun' Mac an Bhaird
Who was known to have built a mortar
In his back yard

Now Ailíll and Von Braun
Were eating bonbons
And drinking champagne
Níl aon ton-ton
Mar do ton-ton *féin*

There's no health plan
For the slightly extended family man
Nuair is minic
A bhíonn a bhean
Sa chlinic

5

For years Medhbh cavorted in the semi nude
On a Celtic Tiger skin modified to self inflate
She lived on the long finger on finger food
Now the Celtic Tiger's head is screwed
Into the wall of a house on a ghost estate
The wall of a house on a ghost estate

Medhbh traded Waterford Crystal for crystal meth
A load of bollix for her metabolic rate
The dual track economy's a duel to the death
Credit card debt came as easily as breath
Even her slate kitchen counter was on the slate
Her slate kitchen counter was on the slate

Medhbh gave up the craic for the crack cocaine
Day-old chicks for cheques she could postdate
She chalked it up to no pain no gain
Now the Celtic Tiger skin is a stain
On the floor of a house on a ghost estate
The floor of a house on a ghost estate

6

You know it's a mulligatawny
when you're drinking Sandeman's tawny
With a guy wearing a *fáinne*
You know it's a goulash
You know it's a hash
You know it's a mishmash . . .

You know it's a salmagundi
When you're standing in your undies
Drinking straight from a bottle of Mundies
You know the job is botched
When you're downing a hotchpotch
Of Ribena and Scotch

And hoping to put the *bó*
Back in the *beau monde*
Down the old bog road
To the back end of beyond

What's much harder to figure
Is what might be triggered
By combining big pharma with bigger
Medhbh's reaction was kneejerk
She went slightly berserk
And jumped into the Merc

She checked the GPS
For what might correspond
To that old bog road
At the back end of beyond

Ailíll assumed she'd be sublimating her aggression
By perhaps planning an indiscretion

Over in Hamilton's bawn
And holding her own petty sessions
With Finbarr O'Ffensive or Pearse O'Ppression
Down the old bog road at the back of beyond

You know it's a salmagundi
When the guy you thought was Lundy's
Been gone for a month of Sundays
It was on Ailíll's watch
That the top notch
Anthrax expert after Robert Koch

Disappeared into the country on which
It hadn't yet dawned
That the old bog road
Is the back end of beyond

7

Medhbh had disengaged the parking brake
Outside Mail Boxes Etc.
Her first call was to Peter O'Paque
Of the O'Paques of Swatragh
She'd mixed OxyContin and methadone
Ochón agus ochón ó
Sometimes one currant adulterates a scone
Ochón agus ochón ó

A Pheadair, a aspail, an bhfaca tú mo ghrá-gheal?
She'd cried to slovenly Peter
Is fearr liom an fear sin ná muire gan smál
He's Zeus to my Demeter
He'll help me out of this hellish zone
Ochón agus ochón ó

He's Romeo to my Juliet he's Darby to my Joan
Ochón agus ochón ó

Some drink the ayahuasca
Down there in Peru
Some drink *uisce beatha*
Moonshine or mountain dew

Some men will give in
To bathtub gin
Some fall before aftershave
But Ailíll is drunk only on Medhbh

Some might play a blinder
With Cecilia or Sheila
And many need a minder
After three tequilas
Some men will concede

To a flagon of mead
Some a sunrise or tidal wave
But Ailíll is drunk only on Medhbh

Some drink reindeer urine
Up there with the Lapps
Some use Honduran
Rum to bait their honeytraps
Some men will succumb
To peach brandy or plum
Some to slivovitz are slaves
But Ailíll is drunk only on Medhbh . . .

Mick Macaroni and Maurice Macabre
Were doing a bit of titration
In their portable meth lab

When they somehow heard Medhbh's ululations
To Ailíll on his distant throne
Ochón agus ochón ó
Medhbh being part-maid part-mother part-crone
Ochón agus ochón ó

8

Ailíll Ailíll Ailíll Ailíll
Ailíll Ailíll Ailíll

Ailíll Ailíll Ailíll Ailíll
Ailíll Ailíll Ailíll

Ailíll Ailíll Ailíll Ailíll
Ailíll Ailíll Ailíll

Ailíll Ailíll Ailíll Ailíll
Ailíll Ailíll Ailíll

9

It must still have seemed all fun and games
To O'Blique and Machination
Though they'd pencilled in their names
In the book of lamentations
Long before O'Blique's cover was blown
Ochón agus ochón ó
O'Blique being Eoin O'Blige from South Tyrone
Ochón agus ochón ó

They talked from both sides of their mouths
They talked so much baloney

Tá sí go measartha tá sí go maith
Said O'Paque and Macaroni
Till the methadone clinic was on the phone
Ochón agus ochón ó
Did they know Medhbh O'Blivion of Ballynemone
Ochón agus ochón ó

Bhí a cnámha sínte i measc na dtom
In the carpark of the Roxy
On account of that omnium-gatherum
Of methadone and Oxy
Her body set off by two traffic cones
Ochón agus ochón ó
Her high heels the only pair of heels she's shown
Ochón agus ochón ó

Now day had wiped the floor with night
Day slumped in a neutral corner
The coffin lid was screwed down tight
And our semi-professional mourners
Struck up their semi-professional moan
Ochón agus ochón ó
For grieving's a skill we can all learn to hone
Ochón agus ochón ó

Acknowledgements

The translation of 'The Churchyard at Creggan' by Art Mac Cubhthaigh (Art McCooey) was included in 'The Drowned Blackbird: An Introduction to 18th Century Ulster Poetry' which was given as the inaugural UCD College of Arts and Humanities College Lecture in 2017.

A version of *The Lament for Art O'Leary*, with music by Jim Lockhart performed by members of Horslips, was presented in 2017 at the Seamus Heaney HomePlace in Bellaghy, County Derry. The role of Eileen O'Connell was played by Lisa Dwan. Art's sister was played by Tara Lynne O'Neill and Art's father by Dan Gordon.

A setting by Scott Wheeler of *Ben Gunn* was first performed at the Albright-Knox Gallery in Buffalo, New York, in 2016. The part of Ben Gunn was sung by the baritone Aaron Engebreth and the pianist was Alison D'Amato.

A version of *Typhoid Mary*, with music by Mohammed Fairouz, was first performed by the Aspen Chamber Orchestra in Aspen, Colorado in 2016. The part of Mary Mallon was taken by mezzo-soprano Kate Lindsey.

Olagón was commissioned by Eighth Blackbird and premièred in 2017 in Chicago, Illinois. The music was written by Dan Trueman and the singer was Iarla Ó Lionáird.